ABC of Ecology

Harry Milgrom

Director of Science
New York City Public Schools

Photographs and design by

Donald Crews

MACMILLAN PUBLISHING CO., INC.
New York

COLLIER MACMILLAN PUBLISHERS
London

32828000029930

Copyright © 1972 Harry Milgrom.
Copyright © 1972 Donald Crews.

Library of Congress catalog
card number:
76-175598
Macmillan Publishing Co., Inc.
866 Third Avenue, New York, N.Y. 10022
Collier-Macmillan Canada Ltd.

Printed in the United States of America
10 9 8 7 6 5 4 3

13779

A atmosphere

Atmosphere is air.
People need a clean
atmosphere.
Smoke makes our

Look outside.
What smoke-makers
do you see?

B bottle

Bottles hold liquids.
Empty bottles left around
make street litter.

Go on a bottle hunt.
What are bottles made of?
What can you do with
empty bottles?

C can

Cans hold foods and drinks.
Empty cans make litter.
Be a can detective.
Test some empty cans
with a magnet.

What cans are pulled
by your magnet?
What cans are not
pulled by your magnet?

D dust

Dust comes from
many things.
Air carries dust
everywhere.

Catch some dust. Spread
butter on an old plate.
Leave it outside for a day.
What do you find on
the plate?

E earth

The earth is our planet. It is like a space ship. It has everything people need to stay alive.

Make a picture of the planet earth. Draw some of the things on the earth that people need to stay alive.

F fuel

A fuel can burn.
Candle wax is fuel.

Ask a grown-up to light a candle.
What does the candle give off
that you can see?
What happens to the candle
as it burns?

G garbage

Garbage comes from the
food and other products
people use.
People must get
rid of garbage.

Who collects your
garbage?
Where does all your
garbage go?

H hydrant

A hydrant is like a giant water faucet. Water from hydrants is used to put out fires and to wash streets.

Make a little hydrant. Fill an empty milk container with water. Hold it over a sink. With a pencil, poke a hole in the bottom of the container. What happens to the water?

I idea

Ideas come from people.
We need ideas to stop
pollution.

Think.
What ideas do you have to
stop pollution?

J jet plane

Jet planes fly in the atmosphere.
Jet plane engines burn liquid fuel.

Watch a jet plane fly.
What do you see?

K kitchen

A kitchen is a busy place. Foods are cleaned there. Meals are cooked there. Kitchen work makes garbage.

What are some ways to cut down on garbage?

L litterbug

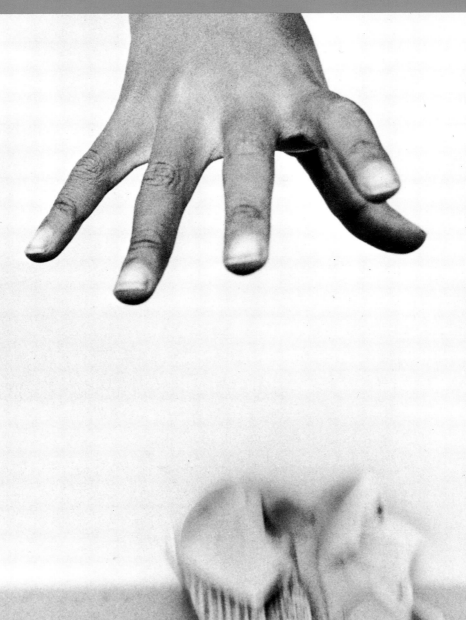

Litterbugs are people.
Litterbugs make litter
everywhere.

What things do
litterbugs drop?
Are you a litterbug?

M mankind

Mankind means all the people on the earth. Pollution kills people. People can stop pollution.

Play a game about people. How are people the same? How are people different?

N noisemaker

Noise can hurt your ears.

Listen to the sounds
around you.
What noises do you hear?
What makes the loudest
noise?

O oil

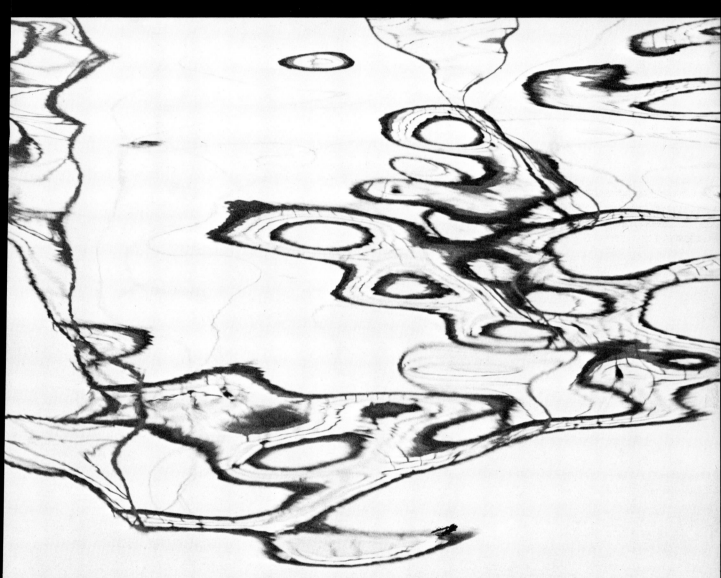

Oil is a liquid.
Water is a liquid.

Put some water in a dish.
Add five drops of
cooking oil.
What happens to the oil
in the water?

P powerhouse

A powerhouse generates electricity.
Some powerhouses burn fuel.
Smoke from burning fuel pollutes the atmosphere.

Go on an electricity hunt. What things in your house run on electricity?

Q quiet place

A quiet place is not noisy.
A quiet place is restful.

Where are some quiet places?
What things are quiet?

R rain

Rain is water that falls
from clouds.
Rain washes the atmosphere.
Rain cleans the streets.

Make a little cloud.
Put water in an empty
spray bottle.
Spray the water out.
What do you see?

S smoke

Smoke comes from fires.
Smoke dirties the
atmosphere.

Be a fire warden.
Where can you find fires
burning?
How do you notice smoke?

T truck

Trucks carry things from one place to another. Many truck engines burn oil. Exhaust gases from trucks pollute the atmosphere.

What kinds of trucks do you see on your street? Where are the exhaust pipes?

U ugly view

An ugly view is not pretty.
Littered streets make
ugly views.
Polluted waters make
ugly views.

Look around you.
What ugly views do you see?
What could you do to make
an ugly view look nicer?

V vacant lot

A vacant lot is land in a
city that is not used.
When a vacant lot is littered,
it is ugly.

Look at a vacant lot.
What do you see?
How would you make a vacant lot
a pleasant place to play?

W water

Water is everywhere.
Clean water helps us
stay alive.

Where do we find water?
How do we use water?

X x-ray

X-ray pictures show what is inside things.

Ask your dentist to show you x-ray pictures of your teeth. Ask your doctor to show you x-ray pictures of chests. What do the pictures show?

Y you

You are a human being.
You want to be healthy. You
must have: clean air—pure
water—good food—sunshine
—exercise—rest—sleep.

How old are you?
Find out about yourself.
How much taller are you
than you were a year ago?
How much more do you weigh?

Z zero hour

Zero hour is the time to do
what must be done to
stop pollution.
What can you do to help
keep the environment clean?

Notes for Parents and Teachers

A atmosphere

Guide children to be on the lookout for signs of smoke anywhere. They may see these smoke-makers: airplanes, automobiles, buses, chimneys, cigarettes, cigars, fires, incinerator flues, smoke stacks, steamships, and trucks.

B bottle

Most bottles are made of glass or plastic. The best way to prevent bottle litter is to arrange to have the empty bottles cleaned and refilled. This is what is done with deposit bottles. Non-deposit glass bottles should be returned to the bottle factory. There the old bottles are crushed and melted to provide the glass for new bottles. The use of old material to make new material is called recycling. It is not easy to recycle plastic bottles. So we get rid of plastic bottles by burning them. The gases given off by burning plastic are poisonous and pollute the air.

C can

Most cans are made of tin-plated iron or of aluminum. The iron in the cans made of tin and iron will be attracted by a magnet; the aluminum cans will not be. Aluminum cans can be efficiently recycled—melted and the metal reused. Tin cans are more difficult to recycle because the tin and iron must be separated before the metals can be reused. If aluminum cans are collected in your area, help your child gather discarded cans and bring them to the depot.

D dust

Dust, dirt, fluff, lint, and spores are tiny bits of material that can come from animals, bedding, clothing, fires, furniture, machines, people, plants, and soil.

E earth

The earth is a huge ball with a diameter (distance through the center from one side to the other) of 8,000 miles. The earth moves through space in two basic ways. It spins around like a top, making one complete turn (rotation) in 24 hours. This gives us day and night. At the same time, the earth also travels (revolves) around the sun in an orbit that requires 365 days to complete. The earth is a vast storehouse. On it are many things that people need to stay alive. Some of these things are:

—air to breathe
—animals for food and clothing material
—clouds for rain and shade
—oceans for food and water
—plants for food and clothing material
—rivers for food and water
—rocks for shelter material (bricks, glass, iron)
—soil for plants
—trees for food, shade, and shelter material (lumber)

F fuel

When fuels burn they give off light and heat. You can see the light and feel the heat. As fuels burn they also give off smoke that you can see. Smoke usually contains carbon dioxide gas, water vapor, and bits of carbon (soot). After the burning stops, ashes often remain. Some common fuels are charcoal, coal, gas, gasoline, oil, paper, wax, and wood.

G garbage

People put their own daily garbage into bags or pails. This is collected every few days by sanitation workers who load the refuse into trucks and cart it away. From the trucks the garbage may be:

1) Dropped into incinerators to be burned.
2) Placed on barges to be carried out to sea and sunk there.
3) Disinfected and used as fill to build up new land areas.

H hydrant

The pressure of the water in the container sends a stream of water out of the hole. As the water level drops the distance the stream shoots out decreases until it stops. In a hydrant the water is also under pressure. Hence, a powerful stream of water will shoot out of a hose that is attached to an opened hydrant. Children should be asked why it is dangerous to block a hydrant with a car or tamper with it.

I idea

Children should be given ample time to formulate their own ideas and come up with proposals for ways to fight air, land, noise, and water pollution. Thus, some youngsters may think of the idea of loading garbage into a rocket ship and sending it off into space. Others may propose digging deep holes into the earth and using its hot interior as a natural incinerator for garbage. Children's ideas should be treated with respect, however farfetched the ideas may seem to be. This will strengthen their idea-formulating capacities.

J jet plane

Jet plane engines burn enormous amounts of fuel to keep the plane flying at very high speed. As a result there is a tremendous outpouring of smoke from the jet. The smoke can be seen as long black streamers that trail away from the engines of the plane. Since there is one trail from each engine, the number of trails gives the number of engines of the plane. Of course, jet smoke adds to atmosphere pollution.

K kitchen

Things that go into a kitchen garbage pail include aluminum foil, bones, cans, cartons, egg shells, fat, fruit pits, fruit rinds, paper napkins, paper bags, paper towels, pea pods, plastic wrap, potato peels, vegetable scraps, and waxed paper. Daily garbage can be reduced by buying beverages in returnable bottles, by using washable plates, cups, and glasses rather than paper ones, and in general by using as few disposable products as possible.

L litterbug

People litter the outdoors by thoughtlessly dropping paper bags, bottles, candy wrappers, cans, used tissues, and other assorted junk on sidewalks, streets and roads, and in yards and parks. Children should be led to understand the important role they have in keeping their environment litter-free. Encourage them to throw litter into the proper receptacles and to participate in local clean-up activities.

M mankind

All people have the same basic physical make-up. All people have fears, desires, and hopes. In these ways all people are the same. People may differ in size, weight, and color of eyes, hair, and skin. They may also have different beliefs, customs, and languages, but all people share the essential needs of adequate food, pure water, and fresh air.

N noisemaker

Children may hear noises that are made by air compressors and drills, alarm gongs, automobile horns, boat whistles, doorbells, fire engines, garbage trucks, loudspeakers, police sirens, radios, railroad trains, snow plows, steam shovels, telephone bells, television sets, and trailer trucks.

O oil

Oil and water do not mix. Instead, the oil floats and spreads out on the water to form an oil slick. When oil spills on oceans, lakes, and rivers, it forms such a slick. This makes it impossible for fresh air to get into the water. As a result, the fish in the water may die. Oil also coats the feathers of water birds and prevents them from flying.

P powerhouse

In most powerhouses fuels are burned. The heat from the burning fuel changes water to steam. The steam hits against a series of curved blades mounted around the rims of wheels called turbines. This causes the turbines to spin. The turbines turn generators. Finally, the generators make the electricity that is carried into homes by power lines. In the homes electricity is used to run such appliances as air conditioners, clocks, fans, heaters, irons, lamps, ovens, radios, refrigerators, shavers, television sets, toasters, toy trains, and washing machines.

Q quiet place

Children may think of such quiet places as bedrooms, caves, gardens, hilltops, lake sides, libraries, meadows, parks, and peaceful valleys. They may think of such quiet things as a fluttering butterfly, a moving cloud, a windblown sailboat, and a falling leaf or snowflake. Noise pollution is a great hazard of our modern environment. Continuous exposure to very loud sounds can lead to deafness and to damage to the nervous system (noise shock). Children should be encouraged to play phonographs, radios, tape recorders, and TV sets at a moderate volume.

R rain

Water moves from the earth to the atmosphere in an endless cycle. Water from the oceans, seas, lakes, and rivers evaporates into the atmosphere. In the form of vapor the water is invisible. High in the atmosphere the vapor cools. It condenses into collections of water drops that we see as clouds. Rain falls from rain clouds and returns to the waters of the earth. Water comes out of a spray bottle in a cloud of tiny drops. As soon as the drops fall or evaporate, the cloud disappears.

S smoke

Smoke from fires is dirty. Smoke may contain tiny bits of black carbon (soot), ashes, sticky tars and oils, sulfur, and unburned fuel. In addition, smoke may be made up of such gases as carbon dioxide, carbon monoxide, nitrogen oxide, sulfur dioxide, and water vapor. Fires can be found burning in forests, furnaces, garbage dumps, incinerators, piles of leaves, power plants, and stoves. You notice smoke because you can see it, you can smell it, and you can feel it when your eyes tear.

T truck

Trucks vary in size from small pick-up trucks to huge trailer trucks. Flat trucks carry bricks, lumber, and other building materials. Tank trucks carry gasoline, milk, oil, and other liquids. Refrigerator trucks carry all kinds of food. Garbage trucks collect and haul away garbage. The number of wheels on trucks can range from four to sixteen. The heavier the load, the more wheels the truck must have. Small trucks have rear exhaust pipes. Large trucks often have front exhaust pipes mounted vertically at the cabs.

U ugly view

Man destroys the beauty of his surroundings when he:

1) Builds crowded cities with too many tall buildings and not enough airy open spaces for people and trees.
2) Crisscrosses the countryside with thousands of miles of superhighways.
3) Cuts into mountains in strip mining, causing irreparable damage through erosion.
4) Dumps waste materials in rivers and lakes.
5) Cuts down forests for timber without replacing the trees removed.
6) Litters city streets and the countryside with garbage and abandoned buildings, machinery and vehicles.

V vacant lot

Children can be introduced to the science of ecology by alerting them to the things and relationships that exist in a vacant lot. Inspection of a clean lot will reveal that:

—many kinds of material (dried leaves, pebbles, rocks, sand, soil) cover the ground of the lot.

—many weeds, grasses, and other plants take root and grow in the soil of the lot.

—many different animals (beetles, millipedes, spiders, worms) feed on the plants and hide under the rocks in the lot.

—rain supplies the water needed by the plants and animals on the lot.

Sometimes careless people dump garbage in a vacant lot. Then the lot fills up with empty bottles and cans, food wastes, and papers. When this happens the lot becomes a breeding place for rats and other vermin. With the cooperation of the lot owner, a littered lot can be made beautiful again in two steps. First, arrange to have the garbage removed with the help of the town's sanitation department. Second, convert the lot into a garden area, a neighborhood park, or a playground.

W water

About three-quarters of the earth's surface is covered with water. Pure water is essential to life. Keeping the waters of the earth free from pollution is one of our most critical tasks. Water is found in clouds, ice, lakes, oceans, rain, rivers, seas, snow, soil, plants, and people (blood, saliva, sweat, urine). We use water for drinking, cooking, washing, growing plants, boating, swimming, and other things.

X x-ray

X-ray pictures of teeth show the extent of decay or damage inside the teeth. Chest x-rays show whether or not a person has healthy lungs. Polluted air can damage people's lungs.

Y you

Help children to understand that individuals are important in the fight against pollution of the environment. Children can contribute in their own small ways by not littering and by learning what they need from their environment to grow up strong and healthy.

Z zero hour

Children should be led to understand that the fight to stop pollution begins at home. Through practice in the ways of keeping themselves, their homes, and their neighborhoods free from pollution, they will grow up to be adults with the determination and the know-how needed to protect their total environment.